This Book Belongs To

_____

Confidence is when you know
you can, and believe in yourself,
like superman.

The End

Be proud of yourself,
but don't boast, and you'll make friends,
and be loved the most.

So don't be arrogant,
it's not cool, Be humble and kind,
that's the golden rule.

We listen and help,
and treat others with respect,
And that's the way, we should all conduct.

When we're humble and kind,
we make friends, And our kindness,
it never ends.

We think we're better,
but it's not true, We're just like everyone else,
me and you.

When we're arrogant,
we push people away, And make them
not want to stay and play.

Arrogance is something
we should never be, It's not nice,
it's not kind, it's not the key.

Arrogance is when you think
you're above, and act like a boss,
with a push and a shove.

Be kind to yourself and
keep trying, And you'll see that
confidence is worth trying.

So remember,
building confidence takes time,
But with patience and effort,
it will surely shine.

Practice self-care, and be kind
to ourselves, These things will help
our confidence, excel.

We should also surround
ourselves with friends, Who support
and encourage, till the very end.

Next, we should speak up,
and express our thoughts, Even if
our voice shakes, it's better than nought.

First, we should set small goals, and
achieve them too, It will give us
a sense of accomplishment,
it's true

To build it up,
there's things we can do,
Like practicing, and
having a clue

Confidence is something
we all can gain, It's not just for some,
it's not just for fame.